BREAKING
the Glaze Ceiling

Sweet Lessons
For Entrepreneurs,
Innovators and Wannabes

Lyle Sussman PhD

ADVANCE PRAISE
for
BREAKING THE GLAZE CEILING

"The most powerful messages for personal and professional success always have and always will be simple, cutting through the clutter of jargon and cliché. This book breaks through that "ceiling" with compelling and practical lessons based on the author watching two entrepreneurs build a successful doughnut business with passion, intelligence and a desire to amaze their customers. (Yes, there is a lot you can learn from doughnuts!) Break through your ceilings, apply these lessons, and turn your customers into admiring fans."

— **Shep Hyken** —
Customer service expert and *New York Times*-bestselling author of *The Amazement Revolution*

"Entrepreneurs are like thoroughbreds—they're born to run. *Breaking the Glaze Ceiling* is a must-read. It is about life-changing experiences and two women who make their dreams come true. The lessons presented in this book are informative, personal, and practical. And "how sweet it is" to learn about entrepreneurship through the lens of two women making donuts. You can nearly taste the pages and the donuts—sweet reading."

— **Dr. Denzil Edge** —
Founder and Former CEO of The Learning House, Inc. and Professor Emeritus, University of Louisville

"Lyle Sussman's great book about the entrepreneurial lessons he learned from his daughter, her partner and Hi-Five Doughnuts is chock full of wisdom and practical tips for a student, anyone in business, or anyone thinking about becoming an entrepreneur. Like a Hi-Five doughnut, this book has a *wow* factor and is more fulfilling than any university lecture or textbook on going into business."

— Dennis McCuistion —

Former bank CEO, Clinical Professor of Corporate Governance at UT Dallas, and PBS TV Host for 27 years

"This book is a quick read that's also inspirational. (And it's always fun to get inspiration from donuts!) Dr. Sussman gives an intriguing perspective that combines the 'ivory tower' of academia and the real world work cut out for entrepreneurs."

— Jennifer Rubenstein —

Board President of the American Independent Business Alliance

"*Breaking the Glaze Ceiling* is an inspiring and informative quick read for anyone who has ever dreamed of starting their own business. Sussman offers great insight to help aspiring entrepreneurs find success doing what they love doing while skipping the dreaded mistakes and pitfalls many business owners make."

— Lesley Pyle, M.Sc. —

Founder of HomeBasedWorkingMoms.com and HireMyMom.com

"*Breaking the Glaze Ceiling* is filled with wise and inspirational advice for entrepreneurs and wannabes. After reading it, I felt that I needed to share it with my children, the entrepreneurs I'm mentoring at the Innovation Center of Panama's City of Knowledge, and my undergraduate and graduate students at my university. I believe the lessons in the book will provide them the courage they need to execute their plans to achieve their dreams."

— **Oscar Leon** —
President of Quality Leadership University, Panama City, Republic of Panama

"Lyle Sussman uses a family success story as foundation for twelve lessons that provide superb guidance for business success. An entertaining read that distills vast amounts of knowledge and experience into a gem of a small book. These breakthrough lessons will have impact for small startups and the Fortune 500."

— **Wayne P. Jones, Ph.D.** —
Former CEO of Pizza Hut International Franchise Association

"As a management and marketing consultant for over 35 years, I've witnessed first-hand the dysfunctional effects of can't-do and won't-do 'ceilings.' Sussman's pithy lessons and applications are on target. They are also entertaining and inspiring. Read, apply, and break through. Achieving really is unlimited."

— **Rex Bennett, Ph.D.** —
Professor Emeritus at University of San Francisco, Author, and President of Achieving Unlimited

Red Letter Publishing, Austin
Copyright © 2016 by Lyle Sussman, Ph.D.
All rights reserved.

Published by Red Letter Publishing, LLC
www.RedLetterPublishing.com

Book design by Kevin Williamson
Cover design by Stephanie Meyers

Created in the United States of America

22 21 20 19 18 17 16   1 2 3 4 5

ISBN 978-0-9981714-7-0 (paperback)

acknowledgements

All businesses sell you something—but very few businesses break through. All books tell you something—but very few books break through. Just as Annie and Leslie, the Donut Divas, broke through, I want this book to break through, both in terms of its conceptual, written message, and in terms of its graphic and illustrative message. My goal is to inform and inspire—to tell you something, but also to encourage you to feel and do something.

From the moment I first conceived this book, I wanted to create an experience for my readers that paralleled the experience created by the Donut Divas. I want you not only to ponder breakthrough lessons from a perspective that challenges your current thinking, but also to experience a visceral, emotional response about those lessons. I want you to feel and experience this book, just as Hi-Five Doughnut Inc. creates a positive experience for those who meet the Divas and buy their doughnuts.

You are the final judge of whether or not I succeeded in breaking through, or whether I succeeded in usefully describing the Divas' breakthrough business. If you believe I have, it's because of the support and talents of some very special people.

The first is my wife, best friend, and personal coach, Suzy. I have written other books, but always as a co-author; this is the first book I've written where I am the sole author. For years, Suzy wondered why I needed or chose to write with others. "Enough is enough," she said. "It's time for you to write your own book." Of course she was right.

But I felt the well was dry. I thought I had said everything I wanted or needed to say in prior books, in newspaper columns, magazine articles, or in peer-reviewed articles. I told Suzy I was tapped out. Focused more on my intellectual fatigue and weariness than by accomplishment, I said, "I've got nothing else to say." With a smile on her face, she said, "Let's go out for a doughnut and talk." This book is the result of eating that doughnut and having that talk. Thank you, Suzy, for helping me break through my ceiling. How sweet it is!

Kevin Williamson is the publisher of this book, but more importantly, the editor and designer of this book. He understood the effect I was trying to create and the quirky, creative appeal of the Divas that I was trying to model. Every author should have a muse; Kevin was mine. I already knew how to communicate to 50-year-old senior executives; Kevin helped me find my voice with millennials. Thank you, Kevin; your creativity exceeded my expectations. You broke through your ceiling.

Stephanie Meyers created the book cover and the donut graphics. She, too, understood my vision and understood the Divas' appeal. In fact, Stephanie is a personal friend of both Annie and Leslie. Stephanie took vicarious pleasure in the Divas' success and was partially responsible for that success (she created their logo). Thank you, Stephanie, for creating images that helped the Divas' break-through, and for creating a book cover that one reviewer said looked "good enough to eat."

Ralph Merkel was my social media maven. We live in a world today where we are constantly bombarded with newsfeeds and digital marketing appeals. Breaking through that noise and creating buzz takes talent, savvy, and creativity. Ralph has shared all three with me. Thank you, Ralph.

I have already personally thanked the readers of the advanced copy of this book who provided blurbs: Shep Hyken, Wayne Jones, Denzil Edge, Rex Bennett, Dennis McCuistion, Jennifer Rubenstein, Lesley Pyle, and Oscar Leon. I respect their accomplishments and am honored by their voices. I now thank them publicly. But beyond this public gratitude, I commit to the following: *I look forward to buying each of you a dozen Hi-Five Doughnuts.*

And finally, a heartfelt thanks to the Divas themselves. As both the form and content of this book took shape, I started spending more and more time observing the Divas in action. I saw the joy on the faces of Hi-Five customers, who would quickly become Hi-Five fans. All I had to do here was describe how and why the Divas could make that happen, then extrapolate those lessons for the public. Thank you, Annie and Leslie, for providing the inspiration to write—and for many of your lessons which I now share with others. How sweet it is, and how sweet you both are.

ABLE OF CONTENTS

DO...NUTS?!

A few years ago, my daughter Annie nearly gave me a heart attack.

I ought to explain right away that I'm a thoroughly practical person—always have been, always will be. I've been a Professor of Management for decades, and I've built a reputation turning the humdrum of business into applicable, actionable teachings: how to address real problems in ways that work, how to cut through cliché and B.S., how to get honest about the possibilities. Over the years I've taught thousands of people how to be practical in this way, but probably none more than my children; they're well-adjusted people with good heads on their shoulders, and until one evening their lives seemed perfectly on track.

Then, out of the blue, Annie tells me that she's going to quit her stable, respectable job to make doughnuts for a living. Not considering it, not thinking about it, but *doing it*. Her tone convinced me she'd already made up her mind—and, at first, that's what scared me.

With these words, Annie was about to embark on a life-altering career path that would test and challenge both of us. Her challenges and tests were, by and large, predictable. She knew, for example, that she would be testing her dream in a world where business failure is the norm and not the exception; she knew she would forsake an administrator's professional salary for uncertain income at best and possible bankruptcy at worst; she knew she would need to change from the 9-to-5 mindset to a mindset of whenever; she knew she would have to work out new expectations with her husband Jason.

But I also faced a challenge and test. At the time of Annie's doughnut announcement, I was a Professor and Chairman of the Management Department at the University of Louisville. Aside from my 40-plus years as an academic, I've also coached, counseled, and consulted in both the public and private sectors. Over four decades, I've helped clients become more competitive in a marketplace where better, faster, smarter, and cheaper were no longer aspirations but minimums.

I've witnessed breathtaking business breakthroughs and heartbreaking business breakdowns. I've seen the joy of people who reaped the benefits of those breakthroughs and the pain of people who paid the financial and personal costs of breakdowns. I've seen families come together under the pressure of starting a business; I've seen families crumble under the same pressures. I've witnessed the "thrill of victory and the agony of defeat."

But beyond my work in the consulting trenches, I chose a career and lived a life that, both implicitly and explicitly, valued formal education. For a few years, my department was called the Department of Management and Entrepreneurship. Chairing that department conferred a degree of expertise upon me, establishing me as a credible and published source on state-of-the-art entrepreneurial practices. I sat on Ph.D. committees, advised Ph.D. students, and read entrepreneurship dissertations.

I mentored student teams on strategies and techniques for improving their entrepreneurial potential. Two of those teams won national new-venture competitions and were honored by ringing the opening bell on NASDAQ, complete with the real-time broadcast on the huge Times Square video screen.

The culmination of those experiences taught me an important lesson:

Unless you are born into a family whose last name appears on buildings, banks, hotels, restaurants, car dealerships, or publicly traded companies, starting a business is like pushing a boulder up a hill—a big boulder and a steep hill, no less.

You are constantly pushing against forces preventing you from reaching the top. You can do it, but it will be harder and tougher than you thought, draining both your financial and physical reserves, and potentially those of your family and friends too. Just how heavy is the boulder and how steep is the hill? According to Bloomberg, eight out of every ten entrepreneurs crash and burn within 18 months of starting and often wind up heavily in debt.

Neither Annie's married name (Harlow) nor her maiden name appears on buildings, banks, hotels, restaurants, car dealerships, or publicly traded companies. I knew the reality of the "agony of defeat" and feared my daughter would experience it. But at the same time, her announcement forced me to move from the confines of my ivory tower and back into the entrepreneurial trenches, where a cherished family member was proposing to act upon what I had been preaching and teaching. I talked the talk; she was going to *walk* the talk.

Even though I came to understand her drive, I was still dumbfounded because baking had never been among Annie's many gifts. I don't *ever* recall her baking a cake, a cookie, or a pie. As a toddler she never made mud pies—and because she was never a Girl Scout she never even sold a box of Thin Mints. She worked in restaurants, but as a server or hostess, not in the kitchen. Imagine a Bedouin nomad from the desert announcing to his family that he was going to become a commercial fisherman. Incongruous? Improbable? *Weird?* On a gut level, that's how I felt about Annie's announcement.

I looked across the dinner table at my wife Suzy, who looked much happier than I felt. I then focused intently on Annie.

"Annie, you have a Master's Degree. You worked hard to get it, and you have a great job to show for it. Why in the world would you quit a job that most of your peers would love to have, and to make…"

I paused a few seconds. "… doughnuts?"

I said it not with anger, but controlled derision. I lowered my voice even further to say *doughnuts*, breaking it into two words and emphasizing the second: dough *nuts*.

Annie smiled, as did her husband Jason, and they looked into one another's eyes. She looked back and me and said, "It's my life, Dad, and I'm not happy doing what I'm doing. I want to go to work smiling, not crying. I've given this a lot of thought, and however it sounds to you, I want to make doughnuts. I know that other towns have weird doughnut shops; I can make it happen here. And I even know what I'm going to call them. Hi-Five Doughnuts."

She got me. Indeed she had a right to be happy, to live her life and achieve that happiness even if it meant shelving her Master's degree and taking a path I would not have taken to sell dough… nuts.

I exhaled deeply. "You're right, Annie," I said. "It's your life. And, you know, I'll be happy to help you write your business plan."

She grinned, and with a wink she said, "Thank you, *Doctor* Sussman. I may take you up on that offer. And by the way, it's not nuts to make donuts." Jason smiled as she said it.

"Touché," I said.

She'd read me right. My response to her donut announcement was the response of a judgmental parent, and a didactic professor and consultant.

After Annie and Jason went home, I turned to Suzy. With a heavy heart, I just said: "Time will tell."

FAST FORWARD

Time has, in fact, been telling. Three years have passed since Annie's announcement. She has yet to take me up on my offer to help her with a business plan. She has never written a formal document that I, or any of my Ph.D. colleagues, would call a business plan. She has never compiled a competitive analysis or market analysis. She has never once used an Excel spreadsheet to analyze "what if" cost-profit scenarios. Neither she nor her business partner, Leslie Wilson, her college roommate and another doughnut neophyte, ever attended a business startup boot camp.

Yet in those three years, Hi-Five Doughnuts, Inc. exceeded my wildest expectations. Annie and Leslie learned how to make doughnuts that people will stand in line to buy, and that companies will order for corporate events. They make doughnuts that customers photograph and post before they eat. They make donuts that appeal to three generations in the same family! Customers will take selfies standing with Annie or Leslie in front of their food truck, Shelby. (Yes, they named their food truck Shelby, after one of the characters in *Steel Magnolias*.)

Their business evolved from a folding table, to a tent, to a food truck, to a brick-and-mortar store. Annie and Leslie were not only selling individual doughnuts at flea markets, but selling thousands at corporate events, weddings, graduation parties, and bar mitzvahs. They are recognized around town as the "Donut Divas." They have cult-like followers who ask when and where their food truck will be parked, and keep showing up to root for their success. The Divas even sell T-shirts, hats, and stickers with their own branding ("If you don't eat Hi-Five Doughnuts, you hate America").

They have never paid for a single ad. Yet they have thousands of followers on social media, have been written up in the local paper, have appeared on local television, and have been highlighted on various blogs. Other entrepreneurs have sensed the Hi-Five momentum and approached the Divas with co-branding proposals.

They even have impact well beyond their native 40202 zip code. They have appeared on national "Best Donuts in America" lists; donut aficionados have traveled from out of state just to buy a "Hi Five." *Southern Living*—that arbiter of fashion, food, and lifestyle—anointed Hi-Five Doughnuts one of the "South's Best Food Trucks."

Wannabe entrepreneurs seek the Divas' secrets for launching a successful business. Imagine: two entrepreneurs who never took a business course, never drafted a formal business plan, and never paid for an ad are mentoring wannabes on the secrets of success. And to put "glazing on the cake," investors have approached them with open checkbooks asking if they can buy into the dream.

With a great deal of pride, borne of amazement, incredulity, and my own personal discovery, I should formally announce that I no longer pronounce "doughnuts" by emphasizing the second syllable.

BREAKING THE CEILING

What did they do that was so different from everyone else? Very simply, **they broke through the "glaze ceiling."** They experimented not only with recipes for the dough, but also with glazes and toppings, resulting in combinations that were weird, inviting, seductive, and above all, chosen by the customer. That's right: customers are co-creators of their own Hi-Five.

The "ladies of the morning" refused to accept what supposedly could or couldn't be put on a doughnut. They even refused to accept what a doughnut should look and taste like. If the glaze and toppings were legal, ethical, palatable, and tasty, you could find them on a Hi-Five. How about a doughnut with bourbon glaze, topped with candied pecans and bacon, or a gravy-glazed doughnut with corn flakes, served by fun-loving women wearing T-shirts emblazoned with "Ladies of the Morning"? Why not?

In the parlance of management consulting, they re-engineered both the doughnut and the doughnut-buying experience. Imagine a fusion of visual aesthetics, customization, comfort food, anti-establishment zeal, quirky humor, creativity, and social media buzz, and you have a sense of what they "re-engineered." They broke through an imaginary ceiling of what a doughnut should look like, taste like, and how it should be sold. The result of this breakthrough is a legion of customers and fans anticipating biting into their next Hi-Five, and telling others about the experience.

And that is the message of this book. **Breakthroughs happen every day in all industries. But they don't happen for all entrepreneurs and they don't happen in all organizations. They only occur if we are courageous, passionate, and focused enough to break through the ceiling—the barriers between us and our creative potential.**

SO WHO WAS "NUTS"—ANNIE OR ME?

Annie and Leslie not only broke through the "glaze ceiling," they also broke through the "it's a dumb idea, it's too risky, it's too costly, I've already got a good job, I'm afraid of failing" ceiling. These are the first limits constraining all entrepreneurs, innovators, and wannabes.

Before she and Leslie launched the business, people would ask Annie if Lyle Sussman was her father; now, people ask me if Annie is my daughter. I talked the talk of risk-taking, innovation, market disruption, following your dream, and seeking personal fulfillment—yet I feared my daughter might actually follow that route.

The evolution of Hi-Five Doughnuts taught me lessons which I once preached but did not fully embrace. Perhaps the most transcendent lesson for me was seeing the bridge between entrepreneurship and innovation in theory versus entrepreneurship and innovation in practice. I witnessed what entrepreneurs could do if courage, dreams, passion, and execution are aligned. I witnessed passion as execution, not just a dream. I witnessed how customers could be turned into fans because of this alignment.

I now share these lessons with all who have a burning desire to follow a dream—

With all entrenched managers who plead for innovation from their team, but have no idea how to foster it in them—

And with anyone who, like me, thought that trading a hard-earned degree and a guaranteed paycheck for an uncertain future was a dumb idea.

Enjoy and apply the lessons that follow, and prepare to break through your ceiling! That breakthrough will not only result in achieving your personal and professional goals, but also validate your worth as a *mensch*—a person of integrity and honor. Breaking your ceiling is self-affirming because you will have achieved your own potential.

Imagine creating a product or service that others will stand in line to buy with a smile on their faces, and a smile on yours, because it's feeding your bank account and soul. It doesn't get much better than that. Imagine leading a team whose passion for your product or service is evident to all. In the corporate world it doesn't get much better than that. Go for it!

My right hand is raised and ready. If you want to break through the "glaze ceiling," join me in a virtual Hi Five. Because who says a Bedouin nomad can't be a good fisherman?

CEILINGS

BREAKDOWNS FOR SOME, **BREAKTHROUGHS** FOR OTHERS

> "It's amazing that more people have climbed Mount Everest than have broken the four-minute mile."
>
> — **ROGER BANNISTER** —
> *first person to run a sub-4-minute mile (1954)*

LESSON

Ceilings—the barriers on achievement, performance, and creativity—**are self-imposed and imposed by others.**

Winners will always break through those ceilings.

The 4-minute mile was once considered impossible. It was the ceiling confronting milers—until Roger Bannister proved it could be broken. When Annie quit her job, she was breaking though a self-imposed ceiling. She was also breaking through a ceiling that others (including, for a time, I) had imposed. Entrepreneurs, innovators, and wannabes are constantly pushing against a ceiling defined by six barriers (more on page 37):

FEAR OF FAILURE The odds are against me. I'm afraid I'll fail and I would be devastated. **LOW SELF-ESTEEM** I'm not good enough. Who am I to think I can make this happen? **SUNK COSTS** I can't give up what I've got. I've invested too much in my current job and lifestyle to let it go. **NEGATIVITY FROM SIGNIFICANT OTHERS** My spouse, friends, and family think it's a dumb idea. They can't all be wrong. **CONSTRAINING COMFORT ZONE** Things are pretty good now. Why make my life harder? **LIMITED FINANCIAL SUPPORT** I'd be starting with no capital!

The reason we revere the Carnegies, Disneys, Jobses, Bransons, and Waltons of the world is not simply that they created iconic companies; it's that we see in them a rare courage, discipline, and tenacity. Like Roger Bannister, they paid a price to create their dreams. They broke through the ceilings most of us live under. They broke through some or all six of those barriers. (You could argue Steve Jobs and Richard Branson broke through a seventh, since both were dyslexic!)

I've watched people stand in line to buy a Hi-Five. Every now and then, one of them will compliment Annie and Leslie on the beauty and quality of their creation and praise their initiative and determination for starting the business. I sense that the people complimenting their spunk and grit walk away thinking, *I wish I had their guts. I wish I was as creative as they are.*

Ceilings are limits and barriers—but not for everyone. They weren't for the Donut Divas and they aren't for anyone who takes a risk and tells naysayers to take a leap, marshaling the courage to overcome the fear of failure.

Kudos to all the ceiling breakers in world. Kudos to the memory of Roger Bannister. Kudos also to every runner who completes a race on a prosthetic limb. Ceilings indeed—but not anymore!

PLANNING ASSUMES
EXECUTION DELIVERS

"Everyone has a plan until
they get punched in the face."

— MIKE TYSON —
9-time WBA heavyweight champion

LESSON

Planning is *do it*; execution is *did it*.

Formal, written business plans are *necessary* to
obtain capital from lenders and investors.

But they are not *sufficient* for
breaking through to business success.

Did the Donut Divas have a plan? Of course they did. Did they have a *formal*, written business plan that would meet the requirements of business professors, investors, or bankers? Not even close. How, then, did they achieve their success without the detailed strategic planning required by business professors, investors, and lenders?

They did the same thing that Steve Jobs and Steve Wosniak did starting Apple, that Harlan Sanders did starting KFC, that Michael Dell did starting Dell Computers, that John Schnatter did starting Papa John's. The Donut Divas started with a dream, a shoestring operation for creating their product, the flexibility and agility to adapt, an acceptance of risk—and most importantly, a **passion to execute.**

Are detailed plans and projections important? Of course they are. Otherwise, my colleagues and I would not teach them. Business students should know about management talent, costs, revenues, market share, and competitive analysis —and without that insight, most investors won't give you the time of day. **But are those official plans and projections enough to become successful? No, they aren't.**

The reason is that **plans assume things will happen and execution *makes* things happen.** All plans are projections into an inherently uncertain future. In any present moment, execution is *ad hoc*, taken one step at a time. You can have a plan, but it won't mean much if you get punched in the face, and if you start a business you will be punched in the face repeatedly. Planning is just contemplation, however complex the flow charts; execution transforms those plans into results.

The absence of a formal plan actually plays into the Divas' strengths. They are spontaneous, fun, warm people; none of their qualities play especially well with spreadsheets, algorithms, apps, or financial projections. Yet their qualities, and the way they use them, have made Hi-Five a success. For the Divas, a Hi-Five donut is an act of love—and serving a customer is an honor they do not take for granted. **The Donut Divas focus on real-time execution and real-time customer excitement.**

The takeaway for corporate execs? Mandating "out-of-the-box thinking" from in-the-box managers is a fool's errand. Making plans without understanding the realities of those who must execute the plans is a *soulless* fool's errand. Spreadsheets and PowerPoint slides conceal as much as they reveal; what they conceal are the sweat, joy, and sometimes tears of execution.

SING *your* SONG

"Alas for those that never sing
But die with all their music in them."

— **OLIVER WENDELL HOLMES** —
U.S. Supreme Court justice, 1900-1932

LESSON

Sing loud, sing clear, and sing while you still can.

A job or career should not be penance.

If your chosen work is not fulfilling, either find
a way to make it fulfilling or choose a different path.

Let's be honest—no one gives 100% effort 100% of the time. We're human beings, not robots. We all have bad days when work can't end quickly enough, when we dread opening the next email, answering the next phone call, or attending the next meeting.

But this Lesson is not about coping with bad days or temporary burnout. "Singing your song" means accepting the reality that you just don't want to fake it anymore, that you're simply going through the motions so you don't get fired. You are sick and tired of being sick and tired, and dread another day on a job that is killing your spirit and soul. You now see Dilbert cartoons as prophetic, not just cynical.

Life is short. **You owe it to yourself to find a job and an organization where you aren't faking it**, where you aren't simply going through the motions for a paycheck. If you believe that such a job doesn't exist, you owe it to yourself to create one. You have a song to sing; either find a way to sing it with your current employer or become your own boss. True, work is a four-letter word, but it doesn't have to be penance.

TGIF—*Thank God It's Friday*—is all too common a sentiment. But for those who have found their song to sing, TGIF means *Thank God I'm Found*. For those like the Donut Divas, who have not only found their song to sing but have an audience who enjoy the song, there's a new joyful acronym: **TGIM**, or *Thank God It's Monday*. Regardless how good your weekend might have been, it is possible to look forward to a Monday because of the opportunities it provides.

The Divas' journey taught me that values espoused are simply words, and wishes. Deeds and actions, on the other hand, are the living proof of those values. You have a choice: express your values in words or live your values in deeds. It's that simple. We have choices to make, all of which have consequences. **We only change the consequences by changing our choices. You can choose to break your ceiling.**

If you decide that you cannot sing your song where you currently work and decide to sing for yourself, make sure every day on your current payroll is one of dignity, responsibility, and pride. Honestly earn your paycheck and you will be able to walk out the door with your head held high. Walk out the door hearing "good luck", not "good riddance." Build bridges, don't burn them. Who knows—the company you quit might be one of your best customers one day. (They may even end up buying you out—it wouldn't be the first time.)

BOOK SMARTS
WITHOUT
STREET SMARTS
ISN'T SMART

"Everybody is a genius.
But if you judge a fish by its ability to climb a tree,
it will live its whole life believing that it is stupid."

— ALBERT EINSTEIN —

LESSON

Degrees and certifications are validation of the discipline,
diligence, and intelligence necessary to obtain them.

But diplomas only get you through the door—
It's performance that breaks through the ceiling.

You aren't *de facto* smart just because you have a formal education. Nor are you *de facto* stupid if you don't. A degree is not the key to entrepreneurial success, nor is the lack of a degree a locked door between you and that success. **Doing always has and always will trump knowing.**

I have served on the faculty of three universities at both the undergraduate and graduate level. Of the thousands of students I taught over the years, who are the most memorable? They are not the students who set the grading curve; I can't even remember the names or faces of most such students. But these are the students I do remember, those who broke through their ceilings:

A **35-YEAR-OLD SINGLE PARENT** working 40 hours a week and raising 2 young children who graduated with a B+ average in 4 years — A **TRIPLE-AMPUTEE VIETNAM VET** who never missed a day of class, even on days when the campus was blanketed with snow and ice — The **ONLY STUDENT, TO THIS DAY, WHO ASKED ME TO LOWER HIS FINAL GRADE** because he believed he didn't earn the "A" that I'd thought he earned — The black student who came to my office after the first class and said, "Dr. Sussman, I want you to know that I'm here because I am the **FIRST PERSON IN MY FAMILY TO GO TO COLLEGE** and I appreciate the opportunity to be here" — the **A+ STUDENT WHO SENT ME AN EMAIL ANNOUNCING THAT "COLLEGE ISN'T FOR ME**, I'm moving to Chile to start a business"

College degrees or certifications should lift you up, not anchor you down. Is a college degree "wasted" when you decide to follow a career path that doesn't require a degree? Of course not. No life experience, especially an educational one, is ever wasted. A degree opens doors; performance breaks through ceilings to get to higher floors. Degrees don't prove you're smart; performance based on astute judgment and street savvy does. If Albert Einstein (the face of genius to many) openly claimed that "everybody is a genius," then who are we to doubt he had a point? But your genius will only be proven when you break through your ceiling.

Though we all have a song to sing, not all of us sing it with the same pitch, tone, or vibrato. Some great singers graduated from Julliard, others never took a single lesson. Some can read sheet music; others learn to sing on street corners.

RISK IS A GIVEN
FAILURE IS NOT

"It is impossible to live without failing at something, unless you live so cautiously that you might as well not have lived at all, in which case you have failed by default."

— J.K. ROWLING —

LESSON

The moment the umbilical cord is cut,
we face a life of risk.

How you view and manage that risk
shapes the quality of your life.

**rum roll please**. **The number one reason why organizations are not as creative and innovative as they could be or should be: they are administratively schizophrenic.** They espouse innovation and "thinking outside the box" while reinforcing fear and imposing negative consequences for doing so. The inevitable consequence over time: disengaged and disgruntled employees who think to themselves, *our company just doesn't walk the talk.*

This corporate schizophrenia is also **why truly creative, out-of-the-box thinkers are easily disillusioned working for large companies.** Giants like Google, Amazon, Intel, Apple, Microsoft, and Facebook aren't worried about recruiting creative problem-solvers; they can fetch the best talent in the world. The bigger worry for those companies is how to *retain* that talent.

Similarly: would-be entrepreneurs experience a form of schizophrenia prior to launching their dreams. They must balance the competing forces of risk tolerance and risk aversion. Entrepreneurs only take off when they reach a tipping point where tolerance outweighs aversion. When Annie announced, "I'm going to sell doughnuts," she was effectively saying, "I will accept and manage the risk." My negative reaction was my own primal risk aversion—a risk aversion which she had already overcome herself.

Life is inherently risky; it requires reasonable diligence. Competition in tomorrow's marketplace requires risk management—setting reasonable odds and making safe bets—but to launch and eventually succeed, you also need an adventurous spirit willing to make bets in the first place. This is true both for the Fortune 500 and the individual entrepreneur.

If we could live life with guarantees, the insurance industry would not exist; nor would locks and security cameras. But how boring would that be? We would never experience the joy of winning, excelling, achieving, and overcoming inherently uncertain circumstances; we'd never win big. Rules may keep you safe (and out of jail), but they don't guarantee success (or permanent job security) anywhere. Living only by the rules is a failure by default, since following the rules doesn't mean you're growing.

Compliance and conformity keep you safe; leveraging risk and asking **why not?** can make you a fortune. The Donut Divas decided they would leverage risk and not "fail by default." **And they broke through.**

of course BREAKTHROUGHS SEEM "WEIRD"

THAT'S WHAT **MAKES** THEM ★ BREAKTHROUGHS ★

"I used to think that anyone doing anything weird was weird.
I suddenly realized that anyone doing anything weird
wasn't weird at all and it was the people saying
they were weird that were weird."

— **SIR PAUL McCARTNEY** —

LESSON

If three people tell you your idea is weird, stupid, asinine, or can't work,
it's quite possible you have a breakthrough idea.

20

"There is no reason anyone would want a computer in their home."
— KEN OLSON, PRESIDENT OF DIGITAL EQUIPMENT CORP (1977) —

"We don't like your boys' sound. Groups are out. Four-piece groups with guitars are finished."
— DECCA RECORDS' REJECTION OF THE BEATLES (1962) —

"Television won't be able to hold onto any market it captures after the first six months.
People will soon get tired of staring at a plywood box every night."
— DARYL ZANUCK, CO-FOUNDER OF 20TH CENTURY FOX —

"Too different from other juveniles on the market to warrant its selling."
— A REJECTION LETTER SENT TO DR. SEUSS —
(BEFORE HE SOLD 300 MILLION COPIES)

There is a simple reason why we label some ideas as "weird"—they don't fit our mental models of how the world should work.** "Weird" ideas challenge our prejudices, biases, and dogma; they unbalance what we know and make us uncomfortable. In 1956, Elvis Presley was "weird" (and dangerous) to most people over 30 because he was the anti-Bing Crosby and the anti-Sinatra.

A focus group is a powerful tool for suggesting incremental improvements for existing products or services, but not for suggesting products or services that never existed. **Trying to think of something that never existed requires a mental model of the world that is weird—that is a deviation from the norm.** If RCA Records had commissioned a focus group in 1952 to create a prototype of a new entertainer, they would not have come up with an "Elvis Presley." He would have been—literally—unimaginable.

I often smile knowing that publicly-traded companies in Louisville are lining up to book a weird doughnut company for corporate events. These are many of the same companies mediating the perpetual conflicts between in-house "weirdos" and "don't rock the boaters."

Ceilings are created by those who have a vested interest in the world as it already *is* or "should be." The weirdos break through those ceilings, disrupt our complacency, and potentially change the world. They always have and they always will. **We can't stop it because we can't ever see it coming!**

> **"**The french fry
> is my canvas.**"**

— RAY KROC —
Founder of McDonald's

LESSON

Innovation is creating something that never existed before.

But so is taking something that has existed
for decades and because of passion and focus **creatively improving it.**

When Annie said "doughnuts," I envisioned round rings of deep-fried dough with **icing**—what you can get anywhere. But I didn't know what *she* envisioned: doughnuts people would stand in line to order, doughnuts that would be a feel-good treat for corporate events and weddings alike, doughnuts with which other companies want to co-brand. In a phrase: she was picturing doughnuts as *more* than fried dough.

Just as the French fry was Ray Kroc's canvas, the doughnut became Annie and Leslie's canvas. **The doughnut is a product and an experience that the Divas reinvented in their own image.**

If "good to great" companies teach us anything, it's that we either get better or we get worse. We must innovate to survive, or else we get locked into status-quo, uninspired humdrum routine and we slowly fade away. Too many managers (and too many wannabe entrepreneurs) view innovation only as the first half of this Lesson, as the generation of brand-new ideas. Too often they ignore the second half and miss the opportunities that are already "started" in the world.

Taking something that currently exists and making it better has created fortunes for many. (Simply look at the shelf space devoted to every variety of paper clip, business envelope, calendar, pencil, and pen in office supply stores—and the variety of frozen french fries in supermarkets.) Everyone in your company could—and should—improve both what you do and how you do it. If they don't, they are simply laborers using their muscles and not their brains. When innovation is the norm and not the exception, tweaking, improving, and refining become just as important as the "eurekas"—and the whole business is stronger for it.

Lots of things have been around a long time—but when viewed as a canvas, and not something that's *already been done*, those **old products and services can suddenly become new and memorable** experiences for both the creators and the customers. Revisit your products or service not as a commodity, but as a canvas. (You don't really have a choice; your competitors are already thinking this way.)

The Donut Divas do not make and sell generic doughnuts; they make and sell Hi-Fives! *Choose a glaze. Choose a topping. Open your mouth, close your eyes, and enjoy.* This is their canvas. What's yours?

LOVE IT
IMPROVE IT

"No matter how well you perform, there's always somebody of intelligent opinion who thinks it's lousy."

— **SIR LAURENCE OLIVIER** —

LESSON

You aren't in business to defend your product or service.
You're in business to sell it.

Rejoice in the kisses; learn from the hisses.

The last time I checked, Hi-Five Doughnuts had thousands of "Likes" on its Facebook page and over 10,000 followers on Instagram. What about the person who bought a Hi-Five whose expectations were not fulfilled? What about the person who did not "Like" the donut, the person of "intelligent opinion" who thought it was "lousy"?

I asked Annie and Leslie what they do when a customer complains about a purchase. Their answer:

> *We never become defensive, and we never blame the customer. We offer a different doughnut*
> *free of charge, or refund the money if they don't want another doughnut. We also ask what we*
> *could do to make it better. We want to make it right and we want to make it better.*

If you don't love what you sell, then don't sell it. But **the dark side of loving what you sell is becoming defensive, and potentially antagonistic, with someone who doesn't love it**—and there will always be someone who doesn't love it.

Truth hurts because it forces us to confront what we don't want to confront. Confront it anyway—for your sake, and for the sake of everyone who has a vested interest in your success. **You aren't in business to defend your product or service; you're in business to sell it.** Realize that a customer who hisses is doing you a favor. Better to hiss to you directly than hiss to the world via the Internet.

Hi-Five's evolution from a folding table to a tent to a food truck to a stand-alone store was the result of thousands of kisses but also a few insightful hisses. Some of these hisses resulted in new recipe formulations and new ideas for glazes, packaging, and marketing. You can spend thousands of dollars on market research; you can also invest that money and ask an unhappy customer a simple and empowering question: *what can we do to make it better?*

Unconditional love is found in houses of worship, in families—and, in rare instances, iconic brands. **A customer's kiss makes you feel good and reinforces what you're currently doing. But a customer's hiss has the potential to improve what you're doing, too.** The Donut Divas love what they sell; they also love turning hisses into kisses. That's how they find a way to make it better. Turn hisses into kisses and you, too, will break through. You may even create an iconic brand of unconditional love.

$ELL THE DREAM THE EXPERIENCE

> " What we sell is the ability for a 43-year-old accountant
> to dress in black leather, ride through small towns,
> and have people be afraid of him. "

— **A HARLEY-DAVIDSON EXECUTIVE** —

LESSON

If the market defines your product or service as
a generic commodity, you will always be in a price war.

**If you're selling a unique experience, customers will
think value, not just price.**

My immediate negative reaction to Annie's doughnut announcement was based not only on my risk aversion (and academic bias), but also because I incorrectly defined "doughnut" as a commodity—not the root of an experience.

Walt Disney had it right when he designed Disneyland. He wasn't selling rides and confections; he was selling experiences and memories. Rides and confections are commodities; memories and experiences are unique. More than 650 million guests have sought those memories and experiences. Today, "the Disney Experience" is even marketed as a customer service training program to other companies.

Zingerman's Deli in Ann Arbor, Michigan also got it right. They weren't selling bagels, lox, and cheese; they were creating "a living culinary laboratory where customers can experience everything from corned beef and noodle kugel to estate-bottled Tuscan olive oil to terrific grits from South Carolina." Their "laboratory" has become so successful that, like Disney, Zingerman also markets employee training programs to other companies.

Marketing 101 in a nutshell: if you can't differentiate your product or service from your competitors, you will forever define your value by price, not quality. Unless you are willing to take a loss to get business, a competitor will always be able to underprice you.

The Donut Divas have not purchased a single ad, but they received local and national media exposure and they have thousands of followers on social media. This media exposure and cult-like following is not the result of selling the cheapest doughnuts in the world. In fact, their doughnuts are priced more like a slice of pie in a restaurant. They aren't selling just a doughnut, they are selling *an experience*—an opportunity for someone to find out why so many people are talking about Hi-Five. They are selling an opportunity to buy a unique doughnut from the Ladies of the Morning.

If you're an entrepreneur and can't create a feel-good experience with your new venture, you may want to rethink quitting your day job. If you're an executive and your product development meetings focus on specs and features, not feelings and experiences, don't be surprised if future quarterly reports are written in red ink, not black. **Never forget: you set the price, but customers always have and always will define the value.**

small data *create* BiG DREAMS

> **"** I won 1,098 games and eight national championships and coached in four different decades. But what I see are not the numbers. I see their faces. **"**

— PAT SUMMITT —
Head Women's Basketball Coach, University of Tennessee (1974-2012)

LESSON

Templates, algorithms, apps, and big data analysis only exist because they are based on small data:

The vitality and richness of discrete human contact—real-time and yet timeless.

One wildly successful entrepreneur—someone who started with a single restaurant and grew it into a successful chain—told me something I now share with entrepreneurs, innovators, and wannabes:

Two bad things can happen if you start a business: you can go broke or you can become very successful. What's bad about being very successful is that you have to hire more people, open more locations, expand your product line, become more involved with vendors and support services, and become less engaged with what made your business in the first place —dealing with customers. This is the Catch-22 of business success: your personal engagement with customers has the potential to create such a success that you become *less* personally engaged with customers.

We are immersed in an era of high-tech commerce. More and more companies service customers through computers rather than human contact. Especially nowadays, **when tech trumps touch**, it shouldn't be a surprise to hear businesspeople say: *I really like the business. It's the customers I don't like.*

Pat Summitt's quote brings us back to reality. **Teamwork and engagement**—whether on a basketball court, the shop floor, the retail floor, under a food tent, or at the window of a food truck—**is based on human beings interacting with human beings.** Eye contact, tone of voice, facial expressions, and real-time engagement result in wins or losses, sales or rejections. Remember: *planning assumes, execution delivers.*

Even though Annie's doughnut announcement sent shivers down my spine, I knew on a gut level that, if she had face-to-face contact with customers, she had a chance to make this work. Annie and Leslie light up rooms by walking into them. That's why their nicknames—the "Donut Divas" and "the Ladies of the Morning"—have stuck so well.

Think about why you've been going to the same hair cutter or stylist for the last five to ten years, or why you've referred others to people like them. Is it *really* because that stylist has always given you the best hair you've ever had at the best price? Or is it because of the small data—conversations, jokes, and the feel-good experience of being served by that person?

The vitality, drama, and richness of real human contact—time-bound yet always timeless—always will break through ceilings.

WE > ME

LESSON

If you want to get very sick, very fast,
launch or run a business without any teamwork or support.

We is better than Me.

Is it possible to launch or run a business without help or assistance from anyone? Yes. There have always been lone wolves. Then again, it's also possible to hit a hole-in-one blindfolded.

Remember, launching a business is like pushing a rock up a hill. You can push it by yourself or you can enlist others to help you push. But **if you push by yourself you will get very sick and tired, very fast.**

The great news about breaking through your ceiling in this era is that the Internet provides you with virtual communities of advisors and investors. What a great time to leverage the We! Don't worry about finding financial support for a breakthrough idea; the world will learn about your idea very quickly, and if it's creative and profitable you will have investors contacting you.

Is a *partner* necessary? Emotional support from family, advisors, mentors and coaches is necessary. A partner is not. Still, even in companies with a single founder (Ford, Walmart, Westinghouse, Walgreens, Dell, Hershey, etc.), success was the result of considerable support from family, well-chosen advisors, investors, and other associates. **The myth of the "Self-Made Business Tycoon" is precisely that: a myth.**

But consider the magic of the right partnership. Consider Bill Hewett and David Packard; Burt Baskin and Irv Robbins; Ben Cohen and Jerry Greenfield; Bill Gates and Paul Allen. In each pairing, would the former have been successful without the latter, and vice versa? If you read histories of these four break-through companies, you'll find the answer is *no*.

In the classroom, I preached the importance of finding the right partners, advisors, and employees. With Hi-Five Doughnuts, I witnessed the make-or-break importance of that advice. The Donut Divas personify synergy, the power of the total being greater than the sum of its parts. With Annie and Leslie, one and one did not equal two; it may as well have been three.

This lesson about "We" also has critical importance for well-established companies. Corporate cultures defined by formal power and status differences, and closed versus open communication, may *espouse* the teamwork mantra but never realize the potential of that mantra. **Breakthrough organizations are characterized by teams of teams, people working with one another, not <u>for</u> one another.** Silos should be found on farms, not in organizations.

DEFINE YOUR BOTTOM LINE

"During my 18 years I came to bat almost 9,000 times.
I struck out almost 1,700 times and walked maybe 1,800 times.
You figure a ballplayer will average about 500 at-bats a season.

That means I played seven years in the major leagues
without even hitting the ball."

— **MICKEY MANTLE** —

LESSON

Every business and every entrepreneur has a bottom line.

**You increase the chances for success and happiness
if your bottom line is more than monetary.**

The Mickey Mantle quote introduces this Lesson because numbers have always defined a baseball player's performance. But those numbers may be misleading depending upon their presentation; they may not capture the true bottom line of that player's career.

Similarly, financial metrics such as ROA (Return on Assets), ROE (Return on Equity), ROI (Return on Investment) and Net Profit Margin (net income divided by net sales) each provide one perspective of "bottom line," but not the only perspective.

Was making money important for the Divas? Of course it was. As Annie once said, "we use dough to make dough." But **the money was not their only bottom line. For them, the bottom line was to have fun** *and* **make money** *and* **create customers** *and* **to spread the joyful Hi-Five experience.** The Divas have been as elated by their social media buzz as by their monthly financial reports. They love posing for selfies in front of Shelby! They rejoice in hearing from out-of-towners waiting to taste their donuts.

If you conducted a focus group of 10 wealthy entrepreneurs and asked them to define their bottom line, you would hear a common response: becoming rich was a *byproduct* of their dream, and not the essence of their dream. The same is true for serial entrepreneurs. The gold ring is creating the businesses, not cashing in for literal gold rings. To quote Einstein again: *Not everything that counts can be counted and not everything that be counted counts.*

Are you able to have a profitable business if your only bottom line is money? Of course you can. **But are you also able to have a profitable** *life* **if your only bottom line is money?** That question is answered every day in every church, mosque, synagogue, and chapel around the world. That question is also answered by every retired executive who works full time for one dollar per year for a school, hospital, religious, or philanthropic organization. (It is also answered in every best-selling book exploring the meaning and purpose of life.)

For accountants, P&L is an abbreviation for Profit and Loss. For well-rounded, happy entrepreneurs, it also stands for Purpose and Legacy. **Not everything that counts can be counted.** Rethink and redefine your own P&L and you will break through your ceiling.

APPLICATION

"We have approximately 60,000 thoughts in a day.
Unfortunately, 95% of them are thoughts we had the day before."

— DEEPAK CHOPRA —

resolving MEANS YOU WANT TO DO SOMETHING.

solving MEANS _____ **YOU DID IT.**

Go to any fitness club next January 2nd and visit that same club three months later. Regardless of the club you choose, you will observe the Law of New Year's Resolutions: Not everyone who resolves to change will change. You can bet your life savings that many of the people you saw in that club on January 2 will not be there 90 days later.

The preceding 12 Lessons provide direction and guidance for breaking through your ceilings. They are the reasons why Hi-Five grew from a folding table to a stand-alone store. They are also transcendent lessons applicable to any entrepreneur, any innovator, and any wannabe. **But they are lessons, not mandates.** Whether and how you apply them is your decision. Will you shatter your ceiling or not?

Your challenge now—whether you are an entrepreneur, an innovator, or a wannabe—is to apply those Lessons, to move from knowing to doing, from theory to practice, from planning to executing, from words to deeds, from *could do* to *will do*, and from whining to winning. The challenge is make sure the Law of New Year's Resolutions doesn't describe you.

The Deepak Chopra quote captures the essence of the application tips you are about to read. **The problem is not that entrepreneurs, innovators, and wannabes *don't think*; the problem is that 95% of the thoughts they have today are the thoughts they had yesterday, and will be the thoughts they will have again tomorrow.**

We are creatures of habit, and unless we change habits, we are destined to perpetuate what feels comfortable even as we wish for a different outcome. The downside of comfort is that it prevents us from doing what is uncomfortable. And let's be honest. If breaking through ceilings were easy, I would not have written this book and you would not be reading it! Breaking ceilings is hard because it is uncomfortable. It tests our resolve, our talents, and our courage.

On January 2nd, gyms are filled with people resolving to get healthy and increase their fitness. Those who remain in that gym 90 days later have abandoned old habits and enacted new behaviors. They were willing to pay the personal price of being uncomfortable. Those who broke their resolutions did not abandon their old patterns and instead opted for comfort.

There are people who want to get fit and there are people who make it happen. There are people who want to launch a business and innovate, and there are people who make it happen. **There are companies that preach out-of-the-box thinking and there are companies that execute out-of-the-box thoughts.** Unless you think differently about what you want to do and how you'll follow through, your tomorrows will simply be recycled yesterdays—and you will forever be a Wannabe.

To help you break through your ceiling and become a winner, consider another law: **The Law of Change. If you always do what you've always done, you'll always get what you've always got.** So, if you want something different, you must now do something different.

Let's begin.

THE SIX
CEILINGS

FEAR OF FAILURE

LOW SELF-ESTEEM

SUNK COSTS

NEGATIVE PRESSURE

CONSTRAINING COMFORT ZONE

LIMITED RESOURCES

FEAR OF **FAILURE**

The odds are against me, you might think. ***I could fail.***

- ○ **You should redefine "failure."** View failure as an opportunity to learn, grow, renew, and expand. A mistake is a teacher, but only if you choose to be the student and learn the lesson. Yes, a startup that does not succeed can still teach you a great deal about reducing the risk in your next venture. You've learned what not to do next time.

- ○ **Use your fear of failure to increase your diligence and thoroughness,** but not to hasten your paralysis or retreat. Fear can be both rational and irrational. Rational fear leads to increased scrutiny and inquiry. Irrational fear will lead to inaction and failure by default. Never placing a bet guarantees that you will never win. Placing a bet sets the stage for a possible win.

- ○ **Failure is an event, not a reflection of you.** The business may not have succeeded; that doesn't make you a failure. *It* failed. But that failure does not define you. Serial entrepreneurs view the marketplace as a gold mine of limitless opportunities. Fearful wannabes view the marketplace as a dangerous minefield. Who is right and who is wrong? Are you seeing a gold mine or a minefield?

- ○ **Change your internal tapes. Edit your self-talk.** Become your own coach and your own cheerleader. You have free will and control over what you tell yourself and why you say it. You may not have control over what others say to you; but you have total control over what you say to yourself.

- ○ **View your life as a journey with many more miles to go** and many more opportunities to leverage. The difference between wannabes and serial entrepreneurs is that the former may never start while the latter will never stop. Never starting and never stopping are both personal, life-defining decisions, either of which you are free to make for yourself.

- ☺ **Start regarding risk as a given, but a given that can be reduced and managed.** Remember the Lesson: *Risk is a given, but failure is not.*

- ☺ Zig Ziglar, author and motivational speaker, said it and it's true: **start waking up to an opportunity clock, not an alarm clock.** Change your language: after all, *alarm* isn't the thought you want for the first moments of your day, but *opportunity* might be. Today is a gift; appreciate it. Start your day with joyful anticipation, not bewildered shock.

- ☺ **Change the ring tone on your cell phone to something that makes you happy.** Are you one of the people who uses the plain, old-phone ringtone? Clean, perhaps, but hardly uplifting.

- ☺ **Read Richard Bolles's *What Color is Your Parachute?*** It doesn't get any better than this—the classic self-help book on finding your career path. One of his major points: If you can't find your perfect job, create it . . . that is, break through your own job ceiling. Bolles also provides self-assessment scales and other exercises to help you measure your strengths and weaknesses as a potential entrepreneur. This career gospel will also help you find your "canvas"- the product or service that ignites your passion, unleashes your talents, and provides the focus for creating your entrepreneurial legacy.

- ☺ **Google the phrase "famous people who failed."** Read long enough (but probably only a couple minutes) and you will be surprised.

- ☺ **Set short-term milestones.** What do you want to accomplish before you go to sleep tonight? By next week? By next month? Short term successes create lifelong legacies. If you are looking for the secret to long term success here it is: **never lose sight of your long-term vision as you set short-term daily goals.**

- ☺ **Subscribe to a daily affirmation blog or website.** There are so many you can choose. Simply Google "Daily Affirmations" and find something that suits you. Getting the daily email, even if you ignore it sometimes, could energize your spirit.

- ☺ **Google "resilience quotes" and find the one you need to hang on.** Sometimes, it's one quote, one phrase, or even one word that channels the motivation you need; it's just a matter of finding it and hanging onto it.

Who am I to think I can make this happen?

- ♻ Regardless of your religion or spiritual beliefs, you can accept this as truth: **as long as you are alive, you have the potential to make tomorrow better than today** and to realize your dreams. This is the underlying story of all successful entrepreneurs, even those who believed they were born with two strikes against them.

- ♻ **If your self-esteem is so low that it's debilitating, seek therapy.** If you believe that you are destined to fail or not worthy of success because of your family background, make an appointment with a therapist today. No one is destined to fail and all are worthy of success. And though many people don't like the idea of seeing a therapist, many of those people need to see one, and they don't realize those sessions could be the best business investment they ever make. Depression and low self-esteem are sometimes compared to seeing the world through a sheet of thick glass; consider that this sheet of glass is just another kind of ceiling to break through. To borrow more language from the mental health professionals, there's nothing pitiful about a cry for help—it's proof that you want to make it, that you're (metaphorically) willing to fight it out with a stick if only someone would hand you one. If you need to go get a stick to fight with, see a therapist; come back to this book to learn more about swinging it.

- ♻ It's not important what people call you; **what's important is which responses you dignify and how you respond** in turn.

- ♻ Ask yourself a simple question: If I'm not happy with my current income and career, **do I choose to simply complain about it or do I choose to break the "woe is me" cycle**?

LOW SELF-ESTEEM

- **Read the biography of Wilma Rudolph**, the triple-gold-medal Olympian who wore leg braces as a child because of polio.

- **Read Laura Hildebrand's *Unbroken***, the story of Louis Zampirini. (You could also watch the movie.) If this doesn't change your perspective on the power of the human spirit . . .

- **Google the phrase "famous people with dyslexia."** You'll be surprised.

- **Google the phrase "famous college dropouts."** (You can probably already guess a few of the names you'll see.) Just as you can fail with a college degree, you can succeed without one.

- **Spend time talking to recent immigrants who started businesses.** You'll be humbled. Imagine: coming to this country with nothing more than a dream for a better life, then making that dream a reality, in the face of obstacles most people can only imagine.

- **Consider contracting the services of a life coach** (but get at least three references before you hire the coach). A tip: don't hire a life coach who has not overcome personal hardships. Find someone who walks the talk.

- **Volunteer your time and talents to any worthy group or groups that need them.** Many (but not all) who are reading this advice have heard the following rebuttal for self-pity: "I felt bad because I had no shoes until I saw someone with no feet." The application tips for combatting low self-esteem are reflections of this self-pity rebuttal. Giving of yourself, your energy, time, and talents has dual effects: it will help you as you help others. They benefit because of your contributions; you benefit because of increased sense of pride and accomplishment. There is a reason why volunteers on Habitat for Humanity projects have smiles on their faces, even when digging ditches. Indeed, **We is better than Me!**

I've got too much invested in my current job and lifestyle.

- **View any investment that got you to today as an investment in tomorrow**, whether that's your time, energy, or money. What you spent is an investment, not a cost. Waste or not, it got you here.

- Put this on a Post-It note and stick it where you will see it every day: **Life is about decisions I make today that will result in a better tomorrow.**

- **Think sails, not anchors.** Any business investments (e.g. marketing, equipment, personnel, research and development) have the potential to reinforce the status quo, thus serving as metaphorical anchors. But investments should never anchor you; they should facilitate forward momentum. They should be sails.

- There is a reason airplanes don't have rearview mirrors. Planes are made to go in only one direction: forward. **Tell yourself that you were born to move in only one direction—upward and onward.** Stop hoping for a better yesterday and stop looking in the rearview mirror.

- **If you want energy, enthusiasm, a can-do spirit, and the potential to disrupt an industry, spend more time with young people (under thirty) and less time with older people.** Young people are still fighting the status quo; older people have accepted it as the norm. There is a reason why most revolutions are started by young people: they have less to lose and more to gain. Better yet, find people over sixty who act think and look as they are thirty years younger. These are the people who fuse wisdom and experience with energy and adventure.

NEGATIVE PRESSURE *from* SIGNIFICANT OTHERS

My spouse, friends, family, or co-workers think it's a dumb idea.

- **Have a heart-to-heart discussion with your significant other(s)** regarding risk aversion and risk tolerance. Perceptions of risk tolerance and risk aversion are subjective and idiosyncratic. Just as beauty is in the eye of the beholder, so too is risk. Probe their feelings. Ask them if they have any regrets about not taking greater risks in their life. You might be surprised at their answer to this question.

- **If your family and friends view you as a failure, spend less time with your family and find new friends.** Spend more time with entrepreneurs. Check out venture startup groups and clubs in your local community. Your Chamber of Commerce should be able to provide contact information.

- **Naysayers and cynics are saying as much about themselves as they are about you and your dream.** Change your peer group from naysayers to yay-sayers.

- Other people are living their lives; **don't give them the power to live your life for you.**

- If you don't have a mentor, advisor, or support group, simply Google "top entrepreneur blogs." 45 minutes of research will help you locate a network of people like you, people who have common interests and help one another without exchanging terms or invoices.

CONSTRAINING *comfort* ZONE

Things are pretty good now, why give up what I've got?

- If you're comfortable where you are, you don't have to change. But if you have an aching feeling that you could do more, and be more, then respond to that ache. **Just know that you can't have it both ways**; you can't say *I like the way things are now* and, with the same breath, *but I'd like to start a business*. If you want to swim, you have to get in the water, even if you feel more comfortable sitting on the beach.

- **Remember that the status quo is self-reinforcing.** It naturally prevents breakthroughs and discourages risk. Stop thinking status quo and start thinking breakthrough.

- The tyranny of the status quo is especially destructive in corporations. Stop thinking *we've always done it this way* and **start asking why you've always done it that way.** Better yet, revisit any policy that's more than three years old. If you can no longer justify it, abandon it.

- **Stop assuming that your status quo will be permanent, regardless of how comforting and profitable it may be.** An entrepreneur somewhere in the world could be, and most likely is, creating a disruptive innovation that will make you very uncomfortable very quickly. Remember: current success is not a guarantee of tomorrow's success.

limited
FINANCIAL
SUPPORT

I'd be starting with no capital.

☼ Great business ideas will always attract capital. **Make your pitch in a way that it can be no-risk or no-brainer for investors.**

☼ **Check out Internet peer funding sources** such as GoFundMe, Kickstarter, or IndieGoGo. Because of social media, high-speed Internet, and mobile computing, business models have evolved from centralized, hierarchical control to models based on decentralized control. We are even moving, in places, from brick-and-mortar banking to peer-funded banking. Remember: We is better than Me.

☼ **Consider bartering as a source of capital.** Maybe you don't have cash, but you can trade your specialty skills or other goods.

☼ **If you have a rich family member, give them the option of becoming an investor or lender.** They may say, *no, but thanks anyway*. Even so, hearing that now is better than hearing *why didn't you call me?* if and when your business takes off. Make sure the agreement terms are in writing even though it's a family member; agreements exist to prevent disagreements, not cause them. Regardless of love and trust, families can be wounded by bad faith and unclear expectations, so put it on paper.

- ☼ **If you decide to seek a loan from a bank or capital from professional investors, you will need a detailed business plan.** You can find business plan templates on the Internet to get started.

- ☼ **Become friendly with a social media maven.** Think social media and shareable buzz, not traditional ads. Better yet, find a social media maven who is *also* trying to break through. That person will have a vested interest in your success and will be able to help you, and you in turn can help them.

- ☼ **Don't overlook your health.** Your health is a form of wealth (you could even say a form of capital). A healthy lifestyle will pay significant dividends when you launch your business.

- ☼ **Develop a lifestyle routine that will allow you to maintain personal balance and conserve your most important resource: yourself.** That means developing routines for nutrition, exercise, stress management, and everything in between. Don't forget that cemeteries are filled with once-indispensable people. Unfortunately, for many of them, money was the only bottom line.

- ☼ **Obtain the services of a business coach.** But, again, get at least three references before you hire.

- ☼ The above tips focus specifically on the individual—you. But **these tips also apply to corporate cultures.** Indeed, some corporate cultures are stuck in a doom loop where both individual employees and their teams believe they are incapable of succeeding and breaking through. They need help. Cynicism and despair are not the inevitable consequence of corporate life. Humdrum, repetitive routine that is never critically and creatively questioned kills the soul and creates an impenetrable ceiling. Courage and questioning breaks through.

- ☼ **Corporate cultures break though the six ceilings not because they talk the talk, but because they *walk* the talk.** There is a very simple test to determine whether or not your current culture imposes ceilings on creativity and breakthrough ideas or whether it shatters those ceilings. This test poses two questions: (1) Do you have a balanced set of goals that define "Bottom Line" to include team work, creativity, and customer satisfaction, and (2) Do you provide financial incentives for achieving these balanced goals? If you can't answer *yes* to both questions, you will continue to reinforce ceilings while hoping, wishing, and even insisting that you do not.

- ☝ **Seek opportunities to be around "weird" people**—not dangerous or crazy people, much less toxic people, but *weird* people. Weird is eccentric and unusual, but often in good ways. Breakthrough ideas are rare in groups of people who think alike, support the status quo, and remain comfortable in their respective comfort zones. This is one of the major arguments for supporting diversity at work. Being around weird people who don't believe in your God or socialize the way you do or look like you, who don't listen to your music or live in your neighborhood or eat the same food may make you uncomfortable at first, but will also prompt ideas you'd never have had otherwise.

- ☝ Where do you find weird people? **You will find them almost anywhere you are not currently frequenting.** Assuming the venues are safe and secure, go to any place that you think is weird, where you wouldn't usually find yourself. Don't be surprised if people look at you and act like you're weird from the moment you walk in—after all, in their eyes, you are. Remember the bar from the first *Star Wars: A New Hope?* (For all you young people out there, that's the first one ever made, or Episode IV.) If you ever walked into a bar like that, you would certainly walk out seeing the bar regulars of this world differently. You can bet a blue lightsaber that the regulars in that galactic bar saw Luke Skywalker and his cronies as weird.

- ☝ Note to all executives in the C Suite: **start spending time with people in your company who you think are weird.** Don't be surprised when you learn they think you are weird. These meetings could create your next breakthrough product!

- ⚬ **Create focus groups of weird people.** If you only ask current customers for ideas on improving your product or service, they will necessarily provide a limited perspective. Their mental models are already shaped by how they use the product or service. Instead, ask a group of 10-year-olds who have never heard of your product or service. Ask a group of newly-arrived immigrants who have never used it. You will be amazed at their perspective; you suddenly have the power to tap a proverbial gold mine of opportunity.

- ⚬ **If you're still in school, take an elective that your peers (maybe even your advisor) think is *stupid* or *crazy*.** This recommendation is a corollary to being around weird people. Electives far removed from your major (e.g. Art History for a Math major, or vice versa) will force you to consider weird ideas, and in forums with weird people—thus allowing you to double-dip.

- ⚬ **Read Roger Von Oech's *A Whack on The Side of the Head*.** This is a fun, easily-accessible book on how to think about problems differently—in other words, how to be creative. If you don't get at least one creative idea after reading this book, you are officially braindead.

- ⚬ Kids work without filtering out the weird. Convene a focus group of kids if you have one handy.

- ⚬ **If a family member or close friend thinks your idea is crazy, don't defend the idea. Probe why that person thinks it's crazy.** Keep asking probing and penetrating questions. Don't defend and don't get angry; simply probe. Either you will get good and insightful feedback or, if the other person begins raising his or her voice and becomes angry, you know you have taken them out of their comfort zone. You can use similar techniques in a corporate setting.

- ⚬ **The three most powerful questions for breaking through ceilings are *what if?*, *why?*, and *why not?*** Start posing them yourself and reward your team members for posing them.

- ⚬ **Shut off your stupid question filter.** The only stupid question in a management meeting is the question people are afraid to ask. Your team will stop thinking out of the box if they think *you* think their questions are stupid.

IF YOU ARE **CURRENTLY EMPLOYED**

The following recommendations are based on three premises:

❶ Your actions should be both ethical and legal,

❷ Your actions should prevent potential litigation, and

❸ Your actions should allow you to exit your current employer on civil, if not friendly, terms.

☝ **Do not operate your business on your current employer's clock or with your employer's resources.** In plain, simple language, that's stealing. The phones, computers, and office supplies do not belong to you; they belong to your employer. How would you feel if one of your employees, without your permission, started a business on your clock with your resources? Remember, when you leave, you want and deserve to hear *good luck*, not *good riddance*. You also don't want to hear *you'll be hearing from our attorneys*.

☝ **Be very careful about using proprietary information from your current employer to start your business. You could be sued.** If you aren't sure about the potential legal implication of intellectual property, talk to an attorney who specializes in intellectual property. Trust me—the money you spend for that advice will save you a great deal of downstream heartache and expense.

☝ **If your current employer asks you to sign a non-compete agreement, seek legal counsel before you sign it.** A non-compete agreement in today's competitive world is common—and prudent. But those agreements are negotiable, as are all contractual agreements between parties. Don't be intimidated, or assume the worst of your employer, if he wants you to sign a non-compete agreement. If your business was successful and your employees decided to quit, wouldn't *you* want the non-compete agreement too?

- **If your current employer knows you want to be your own boss, and you need significant financial backing, set up a meeting to discuss the possibility of selling equity (financial participation) in your business.** If it fits, this could be a win–win for you and your employer. Many startups, in fact, are "spin-offs" funded in part or whole by someone's former employer. If you and your employer go this route, by the way, attorneys are not merely a good idea—they are an absolute necessity.

- **If a customer offers to set you up in business in direct competition with your current employer, talk to an attorney before you agree to the offer.** The customer's offer places you in a legal minefield. Here's my analogy: engaging in an extramarital affair. How would you feel if your spouse cheated on you?

- **If you're starting your business with a current co-worker and you both plan to leave at the same time, try your best to arrange the joint departure to create the least pain possible for your boss.** You want to build bridges, not burn them. You also don't want your boss's anger to spill out in the market and negatively affect your new business. Devote your energy and financial resources to building your business, not to attorney's fees.

- **If you love where you're currently working and would like to buy the company, do your homework and make an offer.** Who knows? The owner may want to sell. But even if the owner says no, you have planted an idea that may germinate. If the owner doesn't have someone to whom they want to pass it, for instance, your offer could indeed result in an eventual sale. To determine the financial worth of the business, talk to your attorney and accountant; they will recommend business valuation experts.

- **To become a future vendor to your current employer, make sure your boss misses you on the day you leave.** You will only create this professional longing if you are both a valued team member and a valued producer. If you meet these two criteria, you not only increase your chances for becoming a future vendor to your former employer, but also increase your chances for becoming a preferred referral if your boss is asked for one. The 12 preceding Lessons provide the guidelines for creating "professional longing" when you depart. Thus, become an innovative, passionate producer in your current job. But remember, if the passion has died, don't fake it . . . move on with your head held high.

IF YOU ARE **AN EMPLOYER**

- Stop your schizophrenic love/hate relationship with your in-house weirdoes.

- **You can't have it both ways.** You can't mandate out-of-the-box thinking if you suppress those who try most to break out of the box. Unless your top management team increases its tolerance for weird ideas, you will perpetuate a schizophrenic corporate culture.

- What's the best way to increase that tolerance? **Realize that someone, somewhere in the world, who has nothing sunk in the status quo, is creating something that could eventually put you out of business.** The most recent evidence? How about AirBnB versus all the hotel chains, or Uber versus all of the taxi companies? If these disruptive, zero-sunk-cost startups can't make you embrace your in-house weirdoes, nothing will. More evidence: In the last decade 65 US companies dropped out of the Fortune 500, while China added 73 companies to that rarefied list. The Fortune 500 list is no longer etched in stone. It is now written in shifting sand.

- Answer this question: **Why should your employees think outside the box if they believe doing so puts their job security in jeopardy?**

- Employers have a vested interested in better, faster, and cheaper (understandably). Employees have a vested interest in maintaining their employment (also understandably). Asking your team to come up with creative and potentially disruptive ideas for better, faster, and cheaper without also discussing the labor force implications of those innovations is a fool's errand. If you can't answer the previous question, don't expect to get breakthrough ideas simply by asking for out-of-the-box thinking.

- **Consider two innovation and brainstorming meetings:** one to focus on out-of-the-box, better, faster, cheaper ideas, and a second to focus on career opportunities and corporate "spin-offs" that could result from the breakthrough out-of-the-box thinking. Your employees should never be asked to think themselves out of a job.

○ Algorithms for filtering unsolicited résumés may exclude future stars. **Develop protocols for finding stars who may not fit the standard mold.** Refer back to the "Book Smarts Without Street Smarts" lesson. You don't want to reject an applicant who might create a business that puts you out of business. True, you may need filtering algorithms if you are screening hundreds of résumés a day. But realize the cost of those algorithms: rejecting an applicant who could break your ceilings and help set you on a corporate path you can't even envision. Those applicants are in there somewhere—find them. If the message of *weird is good* is starting sink in, find ways for recruitment and selection processes that hire 'weird."

LIGHTEN UP—HAVE FUN

○ I recently saw a small sign on the side of a garbage truck—*Complete Satisfaction or Double Your Garbage Back.* Smiling and having fun while serving a customer or working with team members is not against the law. **Who says business has to be painfully serious?** The Hi-Five website says it all: "Everything at Hi-Five is hand-made, hand-cut, and carved out of love." Do the Donut Divas smell like doughnuts at the end of the day? Absolutely. But that's part of their sweetness.

○ **You're creating something that solves a customer's problem or makes a customer's life happier.** If that can't give you any satisfaction, go look for a job as night watchman in a cave. One of the reasons companies hire the Ladies of the Morning for corporate events is because the "suits" vicariously experience the freedom, joy, and weirdness the Ladies bring to the event—and they like it!

○ SOP does not stand for "Standard Operating Penance." Enough is enough. Lighten up. You don't have to turn your workplace into *Animal House* to have fun. You simply have to break the ceiling and realize that **creativity and exuberance are powerful engines that can only add to your bottom line.** You risk losing too much if you don't: unrealized joy in roughly half of your waking hours. And remember a joke at a team member or customer's expense is neither funny nor a joke—it is demeaning and demoralizing, and likely sets the stage for retribution and retaliation.

the
FINAL EXAM

"I think the only advice I can give you on how to live your life well is, first off, remember: it's not the things we do in life that we regret on our deathbed. It is the things we do not."

— **RANDY PAUSCH** —

THE COURAGE TO CHOOSE

Although this book is not a formal tutorial, there is a final exam. This exam, however, doesn't occur at a specific time or on a prescribed schedule. You might take it a year from now or fifty years from now. The exam will be the answer to a simple but profound question. The question determines whether or not you applied the lessons and broke through your ceiling. It's *final* not because you completed a curriculum, but because it occurs at the end of your life.

Indeed, what better final exam can you take than the one at the end of your life's journey?

THE QUESTION

Before I pose the question, consider both the context and rationale for why I choose it as your final exam. The source of your final exam is an Australian, Bonnie Ware, who spent several years administering to terminal patients in palliative care. She witnessed the gut-wrenching humility and clarity people find in the days before they die, looking back on their lives. She asked them: "Do you have any regrets? Do you wish you had done anything differently in your life?"

This, then, is my final exam: **At the end of your life, what regrets do you think you <u>might</u> have? What <u>might</u> you wish you'd done differently?**

Although you could expect everyone to give a unique answer, Ware found five common refrains. Ware reduces her experiences to five themes, which she captured in a powerful book entitled *The Top Five Regrets of the Dying*.

These themes provide anecdotal support for the message of this book: that *breakthroughs happen every day in all industries. But they don't happen for all entrepreneurs and they don't happen in all organizations. They only occur if we are courageous, passionate, and focused enough to break through the ceilings, the barriers between us and our creative potential. Breaking the Glaze Ceiling* used Hi-Five Doughnuts and its phenomenal growth to deduce lessons to help you achieve your creative potential. Ultimately, that potential will only be achieved when you break through your ceiling. The predictable consequence of not breaking through is a lifelong regret.

These, then, are **the five most common regrets, and therefore the most common answers to the final exam.** The best answer one can give is none at all; it is my hope, therefore, that neither these, nor any others, are your regrets on that fated day.

"I wish I'd had the courage to live a life true to myself, not the life others expected of me."
Ware noted: "This was the most common regret of all. When people realize that their life is almost over and look back clearly on it, it is easy to see how many dreams have gone unfulfilled." This regret is the realization that one is dying with their song unsung. Their unique talents were never tested or proven. Their hopes were never realized.

Note the word "courage" in the quoted regret; also note the word "courageous" in this book's message. *You only have one life to live.* You can live it following the dictates of others, their opinions of what is and is not weird, their recommendations of how you should or shouldn't earn a living—or you can courageously follow a path leading to personal fulfillment of your own. What others expect of you is an externally-imposed ceiling. If you succumb to those expectations, the ceiling will become self-imposed as well, and you will be trapped. Indeed, metaphorical ceilings often become traps.

Annie was right: it's not nuts to sell donuts when that was her song to sing. She'd had a professional administrative job requiring an advanced degree, but that job did not feed her soul. She and other ceiling-breakers may shelve their degrees in order to feel their souls, and they are not crazy for doing so. If you don't sing your song, you are setting the stage for the most common regret of the dying to take place at your own death.

You don't have to start a business, and you can fake it at work, going through the motions to avoid being fired. Both choices are yours but understand the inevitable consequence of facing death with your song unsung—you fail the final exam.

As a corporate executive, you too can fake it—pleading for out-of-the-box thinking while punishing those who do so. You don't have to open your mind to weird ideas and challenges to the status quo. But then you, too, will confront Ware's number one regret.

Those who break through the ceiling become heroes to others not solely because of vision, skill, and talent, but because of the courage to live a life of their own choosing, even if others thought it was nuts and tried to push back. With courage, you pass the final exam.

"I wish I hadn't worked so hard."

In Ware's words again: "All of the men I nursed deeply regretted spending so much of their lives on the treadmill of a work existence." At first glance, this regret would seem to contradict my call for courage and living your dream. But there is not, and need not be, a contradiction.Recall the lessons regarding your bottom line and choosing your partners. Of course entrepreneurs will work hard—but that work need not come at the expense of losing family, health, or well-being. Yes, you should love what you do. But loving what you do doesn't mean you should become *obsessed* with what you do. Never forget: the Midas Touch was a curse, not a blessing. Everything King Midas touched turned to gold, including his children. Such a horror story could just as easily have been written by Edgar Allan Poe or Stephen King.

Customers take selfies with the Donut Divas not because they're great bakers, but because they are *joyous* bakers who personify the genuine satisfaction of breaking through the "this is more than a generic donut" ceiling. Just as being true to yourself takes courage, so too does balancing the competing demands of family and business. Those who slow down the treadmill sometimes or ask others to join them on that treadmill will pass the final exam.

"I wish I'd had the courage to express my feelings."

"Many people suppressed their feelings in order to keep peace with others. As a result, they settled for a mediocre existence and never became who they were truly capable of becoming." This regret is an extension of the first regret, not living the life one wanted to live, and the second regret, forsaking your family. You need courage to say "enough is enough."

You need courage to tell your boss, "You're not listening to me." You need courage to tell significant others, who believe your dream is a fool's journey, that it's your journey and not theirs. A song unsung is not only a loss for the person who needed to sing it, but also a loss for those who would have been enriched by hearing it.

If you are a corporate executive, you need courage to listen to what you might find threatening. Never forget: your comfort zone and status quo are ceilings, but not for your competitors passionately trying to disrupt your world.

The donut was a "canvas" for the Ladies of the Morning. Find your canvas and then express yourself on it. When you do, you will pass the final exam.

"I wish I had stayed in touch with my friends."

"There were many deep regrets about not giving friendships the time and effort that they deserved. Everyone misses their friends when they are dying." This regret is also an extension of the three preceding regrets.

Once you realize that the most important things in life are not things (nothing that appears on a statement of net worth), you will be able to find balance. King Midas again comes to mind; riches without others to share them is poverty.

The *We is Better Than Me* lesson applies not only to business partners. It also applies to life partners and to lifelong friends. And remember, friends and associates are not necessarily the same thing. Nor are all the "friends" on your personal social media sites people who will be there when you really need them. Associates and contacts are people you know and who know you. They are not necessarily friends. This third regret is not about forgetting to update your social media sites; it's about losing contact with people who have the potential to make your life more meaningful. They will be there for you, not just networked with you. Think quality not quantity. Think spiritual bonding, not utility. Think We is Better Than Me.

"I wish that I had let myself be happier."
"Fear of change had them pretending to others, and to their selves, that they were content, when deep within, they longed to laugh properly and have silliness in their life again."

If there is a single, transcendent theme cutting across the five regrets, that theme could be reduced to a two-word phrase: **courageous choice**. We have free will and therefore freedom of choice. None of us have control over what's around the corner as we go through life. The only control we have is over the personal choices we make when things happen to us. We, in fact, are free to choose. We can choose to be happier or we can allow ourselves to find the opposite.

They longed to have silliness in their lives again. What a wonderful perspective. Isn't weirdness simply another expression of "silliness"? The Ladies of the Morning rejoice in their silliness, and that joy is an integral ingredient in the dough, glaze, and topping recipes. They have broken through their ceiling and have passed the final exam. Whether you are an entrepreneur, an innovator, or a wannabe, you can and you should too!

HI-FIVE FROM THE
Ladies of the Morning

Leslie Wilson   Annie Harlow

Thank you for taking the time to read the lessons and applications and preparing for the final exam. You may be an entrepreneur, an innovator, a wannabe, or someone associated with one of them. You may be weighing the pros and cons of giving up a predictable income for an uncertain entrepreurial income. Or you may be heading up a well-established company wondering how to rid your company of Dilbert cynicism. Regardless of why you chose to read this book, I am honored that you did. More importantly, you've done yourself a favor by considering strategies and developing goals for breaking through your ceilings.

What you've read thus far is my "voice"—my perspective on how the Donut Divas broke through their ceilings and how I broke through my ceiling. Indeed, when I questioned Annie's decision to make dough…nuts, I implied that doing so was a foolhardy waste of her education and a venture likely to fail.

But these implications reflected my own self-imposed ceiling: a view of the world that said more about me than it did about Annie's dream, Annie's passion, and Annie's view of the world. We all live with ceilings, either self -imposed or imposed by others. The Divas not only broke through self-imposed ceilings, they also broke through ceilings I and others imposed.

Now it's time to hear from the Ladies of the Morning themselves, to hear their "voice"—

ANNIE

"I just wanted to have fun and give people something they would have fun eating. Leslie and I aren't bakers; we're doughnut makers. But we're *fun* doughnut makers, always looking for glazes and toppings that are weird and creative. We're shooting for an experience, not just a doughnut. Our mission is to create a product that makes people happy! We're fun; we're spunky; our doughnuts are a reflection of us. Other doughnut shops sell rings of fried dough to customers . . . we sell Hi-Fives to friends, fans, and followers. It's because of fans and followers that we grew from a folding table to a store.

"We are on an amazing journey. Do I know where this journey will take us? No . . . but I do know we're going to have a great time getting there and we're going to make a lot of people happy along the way."

LESLIE

"This was Annie's dream, and I am lucky to be part of it. We have laughed, cried, lost sleep, cried, and then laughed some more. Annie and I are "people people." We love meeting new folks and introducing them to our doughnuts. That's why we never had to pay for an ad; our fans are our ads. We want our fans to go nuts with our doughnuts. I never believed we'd fail. How can you fail if you're having fun and giving people something they truly enjoy? I loved seeing fans walk up to our truck Shelby with broad smiles and leave with a unique creation— and an even bigger smile. If our journey helps anyone else to follow their dream, our journey becomes that much sweeter."

The Ladies of the Morning broke through because they saw their doughnuts, their truck Shelby, their quirky style, and their inclusive and adventurous approach to life as a way of reaching out and celebrating with people—the essence of what the high-five gesture means. **Imagine creating a business and conducting business as a celebration between buyer and seller . . . not a bad idea.**

Earlier I shared the transcendent lessons I learned about Annie and Leslie's journey: I witnessed what entrepreneurs could do if courage, dreams, passion, and execution are aligned. I witnessed passion as execution, not just a dream. I witnessed how customers could be turned into fans because of this alignment. And perhaps the most important lesson is that breaking your ceiling and executing your dream will transform a working life of cynicism and despair to one of hope and joy.

This book began with my right hand raised for a virtual Hi-Five . . . it concludes with that same Hi-Five. **Here's to your future breakthroughs.**

— **Lyle Sussman**

LYLE SUSSMAN PH.D.

Lyle is the former Chairman and Professor of Management, College of Business, University of Louisville. He received his BS and MS from the University of Wisconsin-Milwaukee and his Ph.D. from Purdue. Aside from 60 scholarly articles, he is a bestselling business author with more than 1,000,000 copies of his 16 books in print, which in aggregate have been translated into 15 languages.

Lyle has taught, lectured, and consulted around the world. His impact as a speaker, consultant, educator, and author has resulted in his selection for *Who's Who in Business Higher Education*. When not in the boardroom, classroom, or ballroom, he takes long and loving walks with his best friend, personal coach, and wife, Suzy— who makes sure that he appreciates weirdness.

HOW *sweet* IT IS

I offer bulk pricing on copies specifically designed for your company.
Together, we can create a custom printing of this book
featuring your logo and a message of your choice.

I also provide consulting, coaching, and keynote speeches to
help you and your team break through ceilings.

To find out more about bulk orders, special printing, or bringing
the 12 ceiling-breaking lessons into your company, contact me at:

www.LyleSussman.com

CPSIA information can be obtained
at www.ICGtesting.com
Printed in the USA
FSOW04n1833310117
30255FS